THE JOY
of the
GOSPEL

GROUP READING GUIDE

to POPE FRANCIS'
Evangelii Gaudium

BILL HUEBSCH

TWENTY
THIRD 23rd
PUBLICATIONS
www.23rdpublications.com

Eighth Printing 2015

TWENTY-THIRD PUBLICATIONS
1 Montauk Avenue, Suite 200, New London, CT 06320
(860) 437-3012 • (800) 321-0411 • www.23rdpublications.com

Cover photo: © Stefano Spaziani

ISBN: 978-1-62785-019-3
Printed in the U.S.A.

HOW TO USE THIS READING GUIDE
Six small group sessions

Gather. Welcome everyone to your group. Offer a special welcome to participants from other faith traditions who may join you. Ask participants to introduce themselves if needed.

As your class or group session gets underway, always begin with the Sign of the Cross.

Read. Read each section of material aloud in your group, rotating readers with each stanza. Pause at each section to follow the recommended group process. Group members should note items in the pope's teaching that strike them as especially important. Do not read aloud the article numbers. They are included to help you find this section in the original document if you want to explore in more depth certain elements of this apostolic exhortation.

Discuss and Pray. When you come to the group process notes, pause to continue around the circle, discussing or praying as the notes direct. Use our suggestions as a starting point and add your own questions, prayers, or action plans.

Six sessions

Finish. As you come to the end of your process, invite participants to identify the one or two large ideas that they hear Pope Francis teaching in that segment of the document. Each participant may hear the text differently; there are no "correct" answers.

Conclude your session with a brief prayer and hospitality.

INTRODUCTION

1 *Those who have a true encounter with Christ find their lives filled with happiness. This is a deep happiness that brings inner emptiness to an end because these Christians are set free from selfishness. They are saved. I want to encourage everyone who experiences this to spread the word, beginning a new chapter in the history of the Church.*

I. DEEP HAPPINESS THAT IS SHARED WITH OTHERS

2 In today's world, we are subject to a blizzard of temptations that lead us away from this authentic happiness. Whenever we become selfish, seeking pleasure and profit only for ourselves, we can no longer hear God's voice. Many baptized Christians are led away from faith by this. They become resentful, angry, and listless. God does not want this for us.

3 So I now invite all Christians throughout the world to pause at this very moment in their lives and allow their hearts to be touched by Christ. Be renewed! Do this daily. I mean this invitation for everyone, and no one should think they are not invited. If you take the risk of giving yourself, heart and soul, to Christ, he will respond each and every time. He never disappoints. His arms are open. Don't ever stop returning to Christ with your whole heart. Now is the time.

Group or personal process

Discuss: What is your experience of "giving your heart to Christ"? How and when do you do that?

....

Action: Pass a cross or other sacred object around the group, person to person. As it comes to each, pray aloud or pray quietly, asking for the grace to offer yourself wholeheartedly to Christ.

---

4 Throughout human history, God has promised that we would find happiness in the Messiah. The prophets spoke eloquently about this. "God…will rejoice over you with gladness," Zephaniah wrote. "He will renew you in his love" (3:17). What a fantastic promise! What tender, parental love this is!

5 Likewise, in the Gospels we read time and again that knowing Christ leads to happiness. Jesus himself promised it. I am teaching you about self-giving love, he said, so that your own happiness may be complete and full. "I have said these things to you," he said in John 15:11, "so that my joy may be in you, and that your joy may be complete."

6 Some Christians live like it's always Lent! They forget about Easter. I do realize that some people are suffering greatly and happiness seems far away for them. But even in these cases, it is possible to live with self-giving love that leads to happiness.

7 Not everything we need and want will ever be provided to us. We should not think that happiness will happen only when everything is in place and "correct" in our lives. In part, this is because our culture is good at providing fleeting experiences of pleasure, but is not very able to help people be really happy. Nonetheless, I have seen many people, even in the midst of challenging life situations, keep a simple faith alive and allow God to reveal himself. Remember, our faith leads to an encounter with the person of Jesus Christ, and that can happen in any circumstance.

8 Only the encounter with Christ leads us away from selfishness and toward self-giving. Only when we imitate Christ and empty ourselves can we know true happiness. And if we have experienced this ourselves, how can we help but tell others about it? This is the inspiration for what I want to tell you in this letter.

> **Group or personal process**
> *Discuss:* How do you hone and refine the art of dying to yourself through self-giving love in your life? To whom are you called to show this love, and how do you do that concretely? How does the practice of self-emptying lead to happiness for you?

II. HAPPINESS GROWS WHEN WE SHARE OUR FAITH

9 Everyone who has experienced Christ in this personal way reaches out to tell others about it and leads them to Christ as well. In this way, the good around us grows ever larger.

10 When I invite you to become part of this, I'm offering you authentic happiness in your own life. Your life has meaning only insofar as you give it away. This is your true purpose and destiny. I ask you to speak about your faith with great joy!

11 The message that we can be freed from selfishness is not itself new, but how we announce it can be very fresh and invigorating. In our culture today, it may sound very new, indeed.

12 And even though we are going to have to sacrifice ourselves for this work, we must also realize that, first and foremost, it is Christ acting through us. We ourselves are loved first by God; it is God's love that we offer to others. God asks us to give up everything for him, but at the same time, God gives everything to us.

13 The work of helping people see how to live in Christ flows from our own memory of having been shown this way ourselves. Remember when it happened to you, that first encounter with Christ? The encounter that really moved your own heart? When you speak to others of this, you speak from that wonderful memory.

> ### Group or personal process:
> *Action:* Create a list of those whom you feel would benefit from hearing the call to follow Jesus, imitating his own self-giving love. Be specific on this list and avoid listing large groups. Try to think about people who live near you, and you may decide to place your own name on this list if you want.
> ....
> *Private prayer:* Speak to Jesus Christ in prayer, accepting his grace and power to be one of those who tells others about the happiness of living with this love.

III. SPEAKING OF FAITH IN OUR DAY AND AGE

14 I write this today on behalf of the whole Church, represented by a group of bishops who met to discuss this in October 2012. They pointed out that speaking of faith like this happens in three principal groups.

15 First, there is the group whom we usually see at worship, even those we don't see there very often. Second, there is that group of people who are away from the Church pretty much completely. And third are those who have not yet met or known about Christ. Many of these latter ones are quietly seeking God in their own way. They yearn for faith. We want to attract them to us by living our own faith convincingly. In this regard, we want to develop a "missionary pastoral ministry" in the Church.

16 These bishops asked me to write this appeal. I have sought advice from many, and I have my own views as well. There are many issues involved, and I can't address them all. I also don't think the pope has the only voice speaking about this; local bishops and others also have a voice.

17 I plan to present some guidelines and write about how the Church can be reformed in doing missionary outreach, certain temptations that pastoral leaders face, how it is that the whole Church must do this work, the role of the homily, how to include the poor in society, our desire for peace and dialogue, and the spirituality that motivates us to do this work.

18 I am writing this to encourage you to invite people and welcome them in God's name by every activity in your life.

CHAPTER ONE

The Church's Missionary Transformation

19 *Christ sent us all to speak about faith,*
faith that flows from his holy heart.

I. A CHURCH THAT GOES FORTH

20 We are all called to go beyond our comfort zones in order to invite others to faith. 21. The happiness we experience comes, like it did for the first disciples, from sharing our faith with others. 22. We speak a word about faith when appropriate, and God does the rest. We can't control how God's word empowers others. 23. Because no one is excluded from God's love, we want to tell everyone about it. We need not fear that we will fail, for God is with us in this.

24 We dare to "stand at the crossroads" of our society and let others see what we believe, because God first stood at those crossroads waiting for us and welcoming us with mercy and love. God has forgiven us and we now help others know that. We want to show God's mercy to all. This happens in people's daily lives; we must get out of our churches and down onto the streets for this. There we patiently plant seeds; God makes them grow. We want to do this without annoying others or driving them away from us, but with warmth, humor, and happiness.

> **Group or personal process**
> *Discuss:* When the right moment arises in our relationships with others, Pope Francis is asking us to speak about how faith fills our lives with meaning. Give an example of a time when you did this in the past, or a time when you could have but failed to do so.

II. PASTORAL ACTIVITY AND CONVERSION TO CHRIST

25 It's no longer enough merely to run a well-managed church. 26. The Church herself must be re-invited to give itself to God. Structures can sometimes hinder us, and we have a lot of structure. Every structure we have must be at the service of the Gospel, or else we should renew it. It was Vatican II that called us to this.

27 I dream of a "missionary option" in the Church, making us more inclusive, more open, and more filled with the desire to go out there and welcome God's people in through the doors. 28. A key part of this must be the local parish. The parish must be in real contact with the homes and lives of its people. The parish is a true community of communities; each home is a place where people can be invited to faith. 29.

Other small communities are also arising today, and we encourage them to stay connected with their parishes.

30 Local churches must always be in the process of renewal and reform in order to stay faithful to the mandate to invite and welcome in God's name. 31. The local bishop must foster this himself. Sometimes he leads, and other times he simply takes his place among the people of God. He must listen closely to his people. 32. I, too, as the pope must do this. I am indeed open to suggestions that can help us all be more effective in our work. The whole central office of the Church needs this reform as well; we have had too much centralization, and I see a need to decentralize the Church.

33 In short, we must all abandon old attitudes or the idea that we have tried something once that did not work well. I call on everyone to be bold and creative in finding ways to invite and welcome in God's name. We have to work together to find the means of doing this! Let's rethink the structures, style, and methods of our work. But in all this, let's continue to work closely together as a single, unified Church.

III. FROM THE HEART OF THE GOSPEL

34 In our day and age, with lightning-fast communications, certain things we teach may be taken out of context or misunderstood. We should not think that everyone understands the background of our teachings. 35. It isn't our task to be obsessed with insistently teaching a disjointed set of doctrines. We must concentrate on the essentials, on what is most appealing and beautiful in our message. The rest will follow. 36. As we taught at Vatican II (Decree on Ecumenism, #11), some of the truths we hold are closer to the heart of the Gospel than others. 37. Likewise, moral teaching also includes matters that are more central to the

Gospel and those that are less so. Works of love toward one's neighbor are very central, for example. Mercy remains the greatest virtue.

38 Those who speak on behalf of the Church must have balance in this regard. For example, if a homilist speaks repeatedly about temperance but fails to speak about charity or justice, he is out of balance. The same is true when we speak more about law than about grace, more about the structures of the Church than about Christ, or more about the pope than about the Word of God.

39 Those who homilize can know they are faithful to the Gospel if this hierarchy of truths is evident in their words. Before all else, the Gospel invites us into a relationship with the God of love; it invites us to see God in others. If this invitation radiates from what we say, we can trust we are near to the heart of the Gospel and all else will follow. If not, our message becomes dry and lifeless.

IV. A MISSION UNDERTAKEN BY HUMAN BEINGS WITH LIMITS

40 The Church herself must grow in her understanding of what all this means and how to accomplish it. We should consult the social sciences, continue to study modern issues, and pay attention to differing currents of thought. Those who want mere doctrine, pure and simple, will find this challenging. But the Gospel offers inexhaustible riches, and it requires various approaches to embrace them all.

41 We are challenged today to restate the abiding truths of our faith in modern terms. As Pope John XXIII said in his opening address at the Council, "The deposit of the faith is one thing...the way it is expressed is another." The meaning of words changes over time and people don't always hear the truth if we use only the old ways of speaking.

42 Having faith always means dying to self, so some people may never be able to accept it. But when people see us living our faith convincingly, they are better able to follow.

43 Certain of our customs have become out of date today; they aren't understood or appreciated by modern men and women. We should examine these and update them. We should not lay burdens on people by demanding they follow out-of-date practices.

44 Those who pastor others in the faith, guiding them in pastoral ministry, should do so with mercy. The circumstances of one's life may have a great impact on one's ability to follow the precepts of the Church. Mercy. Mercy. It is the way we attract others to the faith. This includes the confessional, which should produce joy, not fear. Affirm every small step a person takes, because God's love is at work in people regardless of their failings.

45 Because passing on the faith happens using human words, actions, and situations, we must be careful not to become rigid or closed off. The Spirit is working even in the "mud of the streets."

V. A MOTHER WITH AN OPEN HEART

46 If we are truly a Church "going forth," then our doors must be open. We must not rush out aimlessly, but act with patience when the time is right. Like the father of the prodigal son, we must always watch and wait.

47 When I say that the doors of the Church should be open, I mean that the doors should, literally, be open to allow anyone moved by the Spirit to pray. They should also be open in the sense that our hearts are open to anyone who comes to us. This is true for baptism, but also for Eucharist. The Eucharist is not an award for good behavior; it is a "powerful medicine and nourishment for the weak." We should consider the pastoral consequences of this but be bold in our actions. God gives grace; we don't.

48 If we are to do this work of spreading the faith, there is no doubt that we must make it available to all, and especially to the poor and the sick, to those usually despised and rejected. There is simply no doubt about this.

49 So let us go forth to offer people life in Christ. Teach them the art of self-giving love. I know it will be messy, but, as I have often said to the priests in my native Buenos Aires, I prefer a church that is bruised and dirty but out on the streets to one that is safe and sound, hiding behind its own doors. If anything should bother us, it's not that the Church is bold and reckless in love, but that so many people are living without the comfort of knowing about the self-giving, self-emptying love of Christ. Our fear, if we are to have a fear, is not that we might go astray but that we might remain shut up in our ancient customs, being harsh judges of others, while the people of God wait at our gates, starving for the food we can give them. As Jesus put it, "Give them something to eat" (Mark 6:37).

Group or personal process

Discuss: The chief way we pass on the faith is in our daily lives, speaking of our own faith when the right moment arises. How can your parish support you in doing this?

What do you think are the main reasons why the Church would "close its doors" to people? Talk about both meanings of that phrase.

Pope Francis dreams of a "missionary option" in the Church (#27 and following). In your own words, what does this dream lead us to do and become?

Action: What is your personal reaction to Pope Francis' message in the first chapter? How will you receive this teaching and allow it to change your life? What concrete steps will you take to follow his teaching and leadership?

....

Prayer: Passing the cross or other sacred object around your circle once again, offer a prayer to Christ, committing yourself to speak about your faith and to invite others to join the faith, all in God's name.

CHAPTER TWO

Amid the Crisis of Communal Commitment

50 *As a way of preparing to take up the work of reaching out in faith to others, I want to paint a picture of today's situation in the world and the Church. I do this praying that the Holy Spirit will be in it.*

51 *As we peer into today's society, we must distinguish between what is of God and what is not. This won't be an exhaustive review but I do want to point to certain factors that have a great impact on this work of the Gospel to "go forth."*

I. CHALLENGES FACING TODAY'S WORLD

52 As a human family, we're making great advances in people's welfare, but at the same time many—perhaps most—people are living in terrible situations.

Even in wealthy nations, there is economic inequality. We've learned a lot in these modern times, but we have not yet learned how to share wealth with everyone.

53 When the economic system we follow excludes certain people, keeping them poor, we have to stand up to it and say, "No!" We pay close attention to every move in the stock market, but when our sisters and brothers lie dying in the streets, it's not really news any longer. We stand by while food is being thrown away. Only the fittest survive; those with power want more power. People who don't fit in are thrown away; their labor is used until they're exhausted, and then they're left to die.

54 Many people are tricked into believing that if we take care of the rich first, the poor will get what's left over. This is a false idea. We live rich lifestyles and it makes us deaf to the cries of the poor. We are not moved by the pain of those who suffer; we believe their plight is someone else's responsibility.

55 The root cause of this is that we worship money. Like the Hebrew people in the desert who worshiped the golden calf, we also are consumed by greed.

56 The result of this is that the rich are getting richer and the poor are suffering even more. Anyone who points this out is roundly criticized, but we must say it is so. Added to this is widespread corruption, a thirst for power, and an unending hunger for possessions, as though they give life its meaning. Life is driven by the market.

57 God, however, calls us to live with ethics. This means humans come first and the market comes second. To those entranced by the market, this will sound crazy! God lives above the market and calls us to become all we can be. As Saint John Chrysostom once said, "Not to share one's wealth with the poor is to steal from them and to take away their livelihood. It is not our own goods that we hold, but theirs."

Group or personal process

Discuss: What is your experience of meeting the poor, either in person or by reading about their lives in the news.

....

Discuss: Looking back over Pope Francis' key points above, which one or two of them really stand out as vital and important? Please share why.

58 I urge a financial reform in our lives and in society that puts the needs of others first. I love everyone, but I remind you rich that you are required to help the poor.

59 Much of the violence we see in the world is directly linked to people feeling disenfranchised in their own nations or in the world at large. Inequality provokes a violent response. It appears to be the only remedy to some. Unjust social structures undermine peace.

60 No use of armed force can quell people's drive for justice. An army may put out one fire here only to find another there. We cannot blame the poor for being poor if their rights and opportunities are taken away from them by the rich.

61 Another challenge we face in speaking about faith is religious intolerance in certain places.

62 And yet another challenge is the decline of local cultures as globalization has gotten underway. People become mere cogs in the huge, international economic system. Worldwide media challenge local traditions and values, leaving people rootless.

63 There are also many new religious movements afoot. People often flock to these movements out of the inborn hunger for God. We must admit that part of the blame for this rests with our own parishes. If we exclude people or handle them only with bureaucratic efficiency rather than with pastoral care, they will seek to have their needs met elsewhere.

64 Often religion becomes something less communal and more private. This matches how life is lived in the purely secular realm. But this is disorienting to people since it goes against the grain of what it means to be human.

65 As a Church, we are known for how we care for the poor and oppressed, how we work for peace and reconciliation. This is all very good. Yet, when we raise issues of life and marriage, we are seen as out of touch even though we are following the same moral principles.

66 The family is going through a difficult period of adjustment today to which we must pay attention. 67. Being too individualistic weakens family relationships, which are, by nature, communal. This is true in our homes and also in our society at large, even in the face of war.

68 Our Christian faith survives all these challenges, however. It is deep in our roots and culture. We want to raise that up and make it more prominent. 69. The richness of faith that we seek already exists; we must simply fan the spark into a larger flame. We can face down the challenges before us, whether they be machismo, alcoholism, superstition, violence, or just low Mass attendance. 70. Likewise, we can learn to reduce private devotional life, which prevails among some Catholics, especially when these devotional practices replace authentic Christian ethics. We can coach parents to pass on the faith to their children. And we can reduce consumerism while raising up the needs of the poor.

71 God is present in our whole urban culture, drawing it and us ever closer to himself. He does not hide from us but reveals himself to us generously. 72. People who live in our cities today hunger for God and must find him in the daily lifestyle that unfolds around them. 73. We want to find ways to be present within the city in order to reach people where they live. In the rural areas too, because of media and travel, the same goal exists. 74. Urban areas are multicultural and diverse. There are new opportunities for interaction and relationship here. But while they can become home, they can also become places of alienation.

75 In some cities, people are used, violated, abandoned, and even raped. At the same time, people are connected in important ways to each other because of their close proximity. The message of the Gospel offers hope and love to all, including urban dwellers.

Group or personal process

Discuss: How does our Catholic social teaching reflect the Gospel and the teachings of Jesus Christ? Try to name four or five ways.

Pope Francis is connecting our economic system to the teaching of Jesus Christ. In your own words, how do you describe that connection? What personal challenges does the pope present to you?

II. TEMPTATIONS FACED BY PASTORAL WORKERS

76 I am eternally grateful to all who work for the Church today. I know that we have failed to live up to our ideals, but our contribution to society remains very strong. We help people live and die in peace. We help them escape their poverty and enslavement. We devote ourselves to education and outreach. In fact, the selflessness of pastoral ministers inspires me to give more fully of myself.

77 All of us are affected by the culture around us, and I want to name some ways in which pastoral workers may be tempted. 78. There is a temptation to see pastoral work as "just another job" and to prize personal freedom and relaxation too much. There is also a temptation to reduce faith to a few religious exercises but keep it disconnected from the world. This leads to individualism, a loss of identity as ministers of Christ, and a lack of zeal.

79 The culture around us is often cynical about our beliefs and this can make us feel inferior or foolish in front of our contemporaries. 80. Sadly, this can lead to a real loss of enthusiasm. Pastoral ministers act almost as though God, the poor, and even other people don't matter as much as their own comfort. They lose their way and become blind. 81. Some ministers feel it's asking too much when they're called to bring salt and light to the world. Finding parish catechists today is very difficult, for example.

82 I think this happens because dying to self has gone out of fashion today. The demand for immediate results, even in ministry, overtakes us. We enter into unrealistic projects and lack the patience to wait for the Lord. Sometimes this leads us to be more concerned about our programs than about the people they serve.

83 This leads to a real threat to our task, which is to speak of our faith when convenient or inconvenient. It produces what Pope Benedict called in 1996 "the gray pragmatism of the daily life of the Church, in which all appears to proceed normally, while in reality faith is wearing down and degenerating into small-mindedness." The Church, once on fire with the love of Jesus, now becomes a museum: dry, dead, and life-less. Any zeal is reduced to nothing.

84 And yet, even this situation is not beyond reform! The Holy Spirit is with us. Our faith leads us to get up and get going, to turn water into wine, and to rise up from the tomb. 85. We will not be defeated. We have grace that is always enough for us. We have grace, and grace empowers us to succeed in doing what God wants.

86 Even in situations where we seem to be in the desert, thirsting for faith but not finding it, we can rediscover the power of self-giving love and the happiness that comes from giving ourselves away. 87. The great global communication network in which we live can be turned into a tool with which we reach out to each other. 88. Far from living merely private lives out of touch with anyone outside our circle, we can learn again the art of self-giving, which was the mission of Christ.

89 This is what we are called to by Jesus, to join in solidarity with each other. 90. This requires a personal relationship in which we serve others first. 91. We find Christ in the faces of others. 92. Let us not be robbed of community!

Group or personal process
Discuss: How and when have you experienced the Church becoming dry and lifeless rather than on fire with the love of Jesus Christ?

....

Prayer: Pause here to invite Christ to come into your life as grace; ask for this grace, and open your heart to it. Take the time to write your prayer in four or five lines in order to share it with the others in your group.

93 There is always, however, the danger of "religious worldliness" in which we are pious and churchgoing but still seek mainly our own personal glory and well-being above all. 94. This can lead to either a focus only on intellectualism, or to the insidious belief that we do what we do through our own power, and not because of grace. These latter ones feel always superior to others because they observe certain rules or have held on to a style of being Catholic that is from the past. Instead of leading to love and charity, it leads them to harshness, a distinct lack of charity, and judgmentalism.

95 These people often have an outward show of love for the Church; they may even see themselves as the Church's guardians. But where is their love for people? The mark of Christ is that we die to ourselves. We must return to this.

96 We have to be careful not to wander into carefully planned projects that don't lead to conversion. Conversion happens in real lives. 97. Those who follow this "religious worldliness" often reject the prophetic voices of their sisters and brothers. They distrust anyone who asks questions, and they spend their time pointing out the mistakes of others.

98 The worst expression of this religious worldliness is when it leads to divisions among us. Christians often are at odds with each other! How can this help the Gospel? 99. Instead, we want all who meet us to admire how we love each other. This requires us to die to ourselves, in imitation of Christ. 100. We must avoid all jealousy and enmity between us. 101. We must follow instead the law of love, asking the Lord to guide and empower us for it.

Group or personal process

Discuss: How do you recognize "religious worldliness" in today's Church?

102 Lay people are the vast majority of the people of God, and we know this. The clergy are here to serve the laity. We count on many lay people for their leadership, but in some places, lay people are still not invited or welcomed into ministry. And if they are, their work is all within the parish, but not in the society around them, which is where their real contribution can be made.

103 Likewise, we must acknowledge the huge role that women play in society. In the Church too, women share pastoral responsibility with priests. We need still more opportunities for this. 104. Men and women are equal in dignity, but the question of ordaining women is not open to discussion. We do not suggest that being ordained is more dignified than not being ordained. Service to the Lord is a seamless garment; there are no more-noble or less-noble roles.

105 Social changes have also had an impact on youth ministry. 106. We welcome youth in leadership, and we believe that passing on the faith to youth is a task for the whole community. We welcome their activism and volunteer work, and we want to keep it connected to the Church.

107 We also see a decline in vocations to the priesthood and religious life. We must invite people constantly, but we must also choose candidates carefully. No one seeking power, security, economic well-being, or glory should be accepted.

108 As I said earlier, I have not tried here to offer a road map out of some of these challenges. I want local communities to talk this over and help find solutions. Read the signs of the times carefully. Listen to both the young and the old, seeking new hope from the young and wisdom from the elderly. 109. Let us overcome these challenges, working with true happiness and being bold! Let us grow in our desire to reach out with vigor!

Group or personal process

Discuss: Pope Francis is inviting local communities to talk about and find solutions to the challenges he sees in pastoral ministry today. Return to his list, starting with article #76, and discuss among yourselves how you believe your community can respond. (You may need to choose one or two items if time is limited.)

Action: List the elements that might, for your parish or other community, be part of a plan that helps correct some of the challenges that Pope Francis has named here.

CHAPTER THREE

The Proclamation of the Gospel

110 *Echoing what previous popes have also said, we must make speaking about our faith to a hungry and waiting world our number one priority.*

I. THE ENTIRE PEOPLE OF GOD PROCLAIMS THE GOSPEL

111 The Church is God's people moving ever closer to him. 112. Everything we do, in fact, is possible because God has first reached out to us; now we rely entirely on grace. 113. God unites himself to every human being; no one is excluded. No one can save himself or herself from selfishness. We reach out to the whole world with this message: we can be free because grace moves us toward one another with self-giving rather than self-taking love. We say this to all men and women respectfully and with love. 114. Therefore, the Church must be a place of mercy where everyone feels welcome, loved, forgiven, and affirmed.

115 Humans need to live together in society and, in doing so, form a unique culture in each tribe or nation. 116. Christianity has many cultural expressions of the Gospel. There is much diversity, which is what makes us catholic. People come to faith through their local culture.

117 Cultural diversity produces many gifts for the good of the Church, through the Holy Spirit. When we spread the good news of Jesus Christ, we do not need to also spread any particular culture, such as the European one that has long been associated with it. 118. No single culture exhausts the mystery of Christ.

119 This people of God of which I am speaking is holy because it is anointed by the Spirit. This gives people the capacity to discern what God wants. 120. Each and every baptized person is, therefore, called to speak of their faith and invite others to share it. We become "missionary disciples" just as the first followers of Christ were. Like Saint Paul or the Samaritan woman at the well, once we hear the good news, we are compelled to speak about it.

121 We all need to learn how to become these missionary disciples, learning how to speak about our faith and inviting others to join us. But even though we need such training, we must get up and go now!

122 As I said earlier, we all belong to a specific culture, and it is within this culture that we translate the gifts of God so they can be understood and lived. 123. Part of this is popular piety, which often reflects a local culture very accurately. This piety is one of the treasures of the Church. 124. Pilgrimages and pious occasions of prayer often are a key form of leading others to faith, especially our children. 125. Even if we fail to fully understand local piety, it expresses the deep faith of the people. In our day and age, we should promote this and help guide it. 126. Underlying such piety is the Holy Spirit working in people's lives.

127 Another way to speak of faith is what we call "informal preaching," which takes place in ordinary life on a day-to-day basis. When the moment is right and the Spirit has opened the heart of someone with whom we are in conversation, that is the time for us to mention our faith. 128. We do this with respect and gentleness. We share our joys and hopes, and this leads others to faith. It might be a word, a gesture of love, a sign of forgiveness, or even a prayer. When the circumstances are right, we speak up!

129 Speaking up does not necessarily mean repeating a formula we have memorized; it will often happen in our own words. This allows us to connect to the local culture very closely.

130 The Holy Spirit gives tremendous gifts to the people of God for this work. These gifts aren't given to a few, in order to be enshrined and kept safe; they're given to all. 131. It allows us to bridge diverse cultural situations and create unity among God's people.

132 Another element of speaking about faith is that we must also attend to people in science, medicine, and academic circles. In fact, we want an intentional dialogue with people in these sciences with an eye toward learning how to reach the modern world more effectively. 133. I call on theologians to be in serious dialogue with both science and human experience. 134. Connecting to universities and schools will be very effective.

Group or personal process

Action: List the ways in which the Holy Father teaches us that we can speak about our faith.

....

Discuss: Give examples about how you or people you know

have spoken about faith and invited others to share your faith, values, practices, or beliefs. Pay special attention to the "informal preaching" to which he refers in article 127.

II. THE HOMILY

135 I am going to talk now about homilies and their role in how we invite and welcome in God's name. The faithful attach great importance to the weekly homily. 136. Through the homily, God touches many lives. Just as the people of his time were amazed by the teaching of Jesus (Mark 6:2), so the people today will be when the homily is done well.

137 The homily in a liturgical setting is not the same as giving a lesson or pausing to meditate. It's more of a dialogue: the preacher speaking from the heart of the community about the heart of God. 138. It's not a form of entertainment but it does need to reach people. It should be brief and powerful enough to change lives.

139 The homilist is like a mother who understands her children well, speaks to them from her heart, listens to their concerns, and guides them to fuller life. 140. Hence the tone and warmth of the preacher is important, and his happiness must be evident. 141. In just the same way, Jesus taught from his heart and spoke to the hearts of the people of his time.

142 Again, the homily is heart-to-heart communication. If it becomes a lecture, a scolding, a moral tome, or a doctrinal thesis, it does not do this. 143. The Lord and his people speak to one another in many ways each day in prayer, but the homily serves as an instrument to both enlighten and promote this.

144 To speak from the heart means that our hearts must be on fire, which is the key characteristic of a good preacher.

III. PREPARING TO PREACH

145 I am going to suggest now a method for preparing the homily. 146. First ask the Spirit to guide you. Then give full attention to the text. Be full of awe and reverence for it.

147 This may seem obvious, but I want to insist that preachers read good commentaries on the text. These words are two or three thousand years old, after all, and we must plumb them to gain their meaning. 148. Be careful not to take one or another line of Scripture out of the context of the whole Bible. God is revealing God's own self here, not a collection of maxims or details.

149 Next, the preacher should make the word his or her own. Let it speak to your heart; share it with others; allow its power to engulf you. 150. Make sure you don't use the text to demand of others what you yourself do not live. 151. As a preacher you must be aware that God loves you, and this must be clear to your listeners. The word has to touch your own life, or how can you expect it to touch others?

152 I suggest using *lectio divina* as you prepare. This is a prayerful way to read the Bible in which you pay attention to how the Lord is speaking to you in the text. 153. Pay attention to how a particular text moves you, disturbs you, or even attracts you.

154 Now turn your ear to your people. Pay attention to what the community needs to hear, in this culture and in this time. Link the message to the real world around you. 155. You must have profound sensitivity to what affects people on a day-to-day basis.

155 It's not enough to know what should be said if you don't know how to speak so people can really hear you. Don't let too much content overwhelm your core message. 157. Use images, for example, to illustrate a point. Help them savor the message and desire God. 158. Keep it simple, clear, and direct. Terms used to study theology don't make very good terms in a homily. Use common words.

159 Keep the homily positive. Offer hope, not criticism. Work together as a community to make preaching always more positive and powerful!

> **Group or personal process**
> *Discuss:* What strikes you as most important in the discussion of homilies presented here by Pope Francis? Why do you think he spent so much time on this aspect of evangelization?

IV. EVANGELIZATION AND THE DEEPER UNDERSTANDING OF THE *KERYGMA*

160 We don't just announce the good news, speak of faith, and welcome others. We also set ourselves on a pathway to grow in our faith. 161. This isn't mere growth in doctrinal understanding, but it is also learning a "way of love." Love is the heart of the Gospel. It fulfills the law. 162. God gives us the gift of grace and it is only by grace that we can grow in love.

163 Faith formation and catechesis help make this growth possible, and we have several recent documents on this, which I need not repeat. But I do have several thoughts about it all.

164 We refer to the announcement of the core message of Jesus Christ as the *kerygma*. The first words every teacher and catechist must utter, therefore, are this same announcement: "Jesus loves you; his self-emptying death on the cross saves you from selfishness and sin; now he walks with you every day."

165 There is a temptation to think that once we announce this core message, we can get onto more important catechetical work. Actually, this *kerygma* is the more important work and nothing surpasses it in importance. Our announcement of it must be warm, welcoming, and non-judgmental.

Group or personal process
Discuss: In your own words, what does the term *kerygma* mean? How do you experience it in your life and how do you speak about it to others?

166 We also speak of *mystagogy*, and by it we mean "looking back over our shoulder" at celebrations, encounters with people, or events that have just happened in order to see the hand of God in them. This is one way people come to know and recognize God in their midst.

167 It goes without saying that beauty and the arts play a major role in this. God speaks through them to touch us in ways mere words cannot. 168. In all of this, we leaders must be happy and positive messengers of good news, not dour delivery persons of judgment and dire warnings.

169 We should remember that our task is to accompany others on their journeys of faith, and to be accompanied ourselves by others. That we accompany others gives us a sacred role. 170. Obvious as this seems, we accompany them in order to lead them to God, so anyone on the journey must have this goal in mind. 171. This requires that we listen to them and enter into their lives and growth. This demands patience on our part because people grow step-by-step toward the mystery of God.

172 Anyone who walks the journey of faith with another must realize that how God's grace is at work in this person's life is a mystery in part. 173. In the end, the goal of everything, even one's early steps on the journey of faith, is service of others.

174 Central to all work toward inviting and welcoming, toward speaking clearly about our faith to others, is Scripture itself. The word of God is at our center. 175. Because of this, we must make the word available to all. God has indeed spoken to us in Scripture; we receive and share it as a treasure.

> ### Group or personal process
> *Discuss:* You have been invited to speak about your faith and invite others to join you in it. Your audience is a group of people who are modern urban citizens of your own nation, but have not heard about Jesus or the Gospel before this. What will you tell them?

CHAPTER FOUR

The Social Dimension of Evangelization

176 *To speak about our own faith and invite others to share it builds the kingdom of God on earth. To be authentic, however, we must not omit any dimension of this task, and I now want to express some concerns about the social dimensions of evangelization.*

I. COMMUNAL AND SOCIETAL REPERCUSSIONS OF THE *KERYGMA*

177 When we defined the term *kerygma* earlier, we said it reflected the core message of Jesus Christ, which always leads to love. Therein we find the social dimension: love and charity.

178 That God loves all women and men means that all men and women have dignity. When we are saved from selfishness, this is a reference to the social dimension. One is not selfish unless he or she takes from another, withholds from another, or fails to love another. Christ loves us. Love is social by definition. We desire, seek, and protect the well-being of others because of God's love for us.

179 The Scriptures teach us this over and over again. In the most dramatic way, we are reminded that whatever we do (or fail to do) for the least among us is what we do (or fail to do) to Christ himself. We cannot preach the Gospel unless we preach the love of others at the same time.

180 The message of Christ is about the community of God, of which we are all a part. We are the people of God. 181. The task of proclaiming the good news of Jesus Christ is meant for everyone. Within it is a mandate for charity, and this reaches all levels of existence, all people, and all aspects of community life.

182 Religion is not a private matter, but a social one. God wants all people to be happy in this world as well as eternally. 183. Real faith desires to change the world, not to make everyone follow the same creed, but so that everyone can live with justice and peace.

184 I don't plan to comment on specific social questions. Neither the pope nor the Church knows all the answers to those. We want the local community to analyze their own situations. 185. But I do want to comment on two areas: the poor in society, and peace and social dialogue.

Group or personal process
Discuss: Summarize the main points in the section you just read. Review it now and identify the key thoughts expressed by Pope Francis.

II. THE INCLUSION OF THE POOR IN SOCIETY

186 We are concerned for the poor because we believe in Christ, who was poor himself. 187. The liberation and promotion of the poor is a task that belongs to all the followers of Christ. The Scriptures lead us to believe this. 188. The cry for justice that rises from the poor cannot be ignored by us. Jesus himself told us, "You give them something to eat" (Mark 6:37).

189 We are called, on a deep level, to be in solidarity with the poor. Our attitude must change so that we begin to see everything as shared. 190. Our own rights are valid only insofar that we understand that the earth belongs to all humankind, not to a lucky few. 191. All Christians are called to hear the cry of the poor. We know there is enough food for all on earth, yet poor distribution, wastefulness, and corruption prevent everyone from being fed. 192. Beyond food, we also believe everyone should have education, health care, and employment.

193 We must be deeply moved by the suffering of others. Such empathy will lead us to have mercy on them, even at personal sacrifice to ourselves. 194. This is not terribly complicated. We are called to humble service of each other, to love one another, and to have justice and mercy toward the poor. It's that simple. 195. In the early Church, authentic faith was determined by how well the poor were treated (Galatians 2:10). 196. Hardness of heart in this regard leads to the breakdown of society.

197 Remember that Mary was a lowly maiden from a small town on the edge of the empire. Jesus was born in a stable. When he was presented at the Temple, doves were the gift because the family could not afford a lamb. His message was addressed to the poor first.

198 I want a poor church that is for the poor because they have much to teach us. It's fundamental to our faith. We are called to see Christ in the poor and minister to him there. 199. We must allow our own hearts to be touched by them, to become their friends, to find them beautiful, and to allow them to lead us closer to the heart of the Lord.

200 As a Church we must offer the poor better pastoral care. 201. And no one should think that he or she is not called to this work. It's part and parcel of our faith. I'm not asking for a mere intellectual agreement, but for people at every level of the Church to roll up their sleeves and get busy.

202 We also need to correct the structural problems in our economic systems that keep the poor enslaved. This is urgent in order to avoid further violence and war. This inequality is the root of all social ills. 203. Affirming and supporting human dignity should be the aim of every economic system. But when we raise the idea of ethics, people are irked by it. It gets in the way of profit. 204. The so-called "unseen hand" that should guide economic systems is a myth. We need political solutions that work instead.

205 Let us pray for politicians who have a heart for the poor. Politics can be a lofty vocation if charity rules it. 206. In order to have a global community in which all are cared for, we need an efficient way of communicating about this while maintaining the sovereignty of each nation.

207 All Christian communities in the world share this responsibility. 208. I mean to offend no one with these words; I am not your foe but your partner in this endeavor. 209. We must care for the vulnerable, as Christ did. 210. Today people are made vulnerable in new ways: immigrants, refugees, and the elderly, to name a few. 211. Not to mention exploiting the young for sex or money; you can't look away from this and make it go away. It is the ugly truth. 212. In addition, we often see women become nearly powerless victims of violence.

213 The Church also has great love and concern for unborn children who are denied their dignity, as though they were not conceived. 214. We will not change our teaching here. It should not be considered "progressive" to eliminate a human life. We must also do a better job of accompanying women in difficult pregnancies.

215 I think also about the pain of the earth itself as it is exploited and ruined through our desire for power or money. Today in places, the earth is a wasteland. 216. We must protect our fragile earth.

Group or personal process

Discuss: Describe how you as a parish or other community (or even as a household) will take concrete steps to include the poor and vulnerable and be in greater solidarity with them. Be quite specific.

....

Prayer: Create a prayer in which you offer your own money, property, and possessions to Christ to use as needed for his mission.

III. THE COMMON GOOD AND PEACE IN SOCIETY

217 Peace produces many fruits for the human family. 218. Lasting peace does not result from keeping the poor quiet while the rich enjoy their lifestyles. It results from a fair distribution of opportunities and goods. 219. Nor is peace merely the absence of war based on a so-called "balance of power." This isn't peace; it's a life lived in fear that the balance will tip. 220. Peace is built up by every generation as cooperation and fair distribution become part of society. 221. Such a building up of peace rests on four pillars, which I want to examine out of the conviction that following them can lead to world peace.

222 The first principle is that long-term plans unfold at their own pace even if short-term gains elude us. 223. This means that over time our initiatives will succeed even if the result is not immediate. We must get started with a plan to remedy our out-of-balance distribution of goods; we must be convinced of the long-term goal. 224. I know some people today think mainly about obtaining immediate results in order to assure short-term political gains. 225. This principle also applies to spreading the good news of our faith.

226 We know there is conflict among nations and peoples, but the second principle leads us to believe that underneath it all is a stronger sense of unity. 227. Some people see conflict and ignore it. Others become swamped by it. A third option is to confront it and use it to build a better society. 228. This latter approach requires great people with noble hearts who can hold unity as a value in the midst of conflict. It leads to resolutions that respect the dignity of all parties. 229. Such unity is God's idea expressed throughout the Scriptures. 230. This principle leads, not to a mere negotiated settlement, but to peace based on compromise and harmony even in the midst of diversity.

231 The third principle is that reality exists but ideas are always developing. We cannot dwell only in the realm of talk and words. At some point, we have to get down to business and deal with the reality of what's there. Realities, we argue, are greater than ideas. 232. If we allow ideas to rule, we end up without action. A mere logical proposal means nothing if it doesn't lead to a remedy for the reality people face. 233. The theology of love and justice that I have been articulating is not a mere idea. Jesus Christ is incarnate in reality. We must put the word into practice or we will become dry and lifeless.

234 The final principle is that the whole is greater than the part. This means that we must broaden our horizons. We keep our eye on the global needs while continuing to work on local ones. 235. Keeping our eye on the result for humanity of our efforts for justice and peace allows us to see beyond the particular place in which we work. It gives us hope, direction, and purpose. 236. There is a place for everyone in working toward this great goal, and each has his or her particular task. 237. Just as around the world we are of many cultures but still we are the one people of God, so our efforts for peace gather together for one great cause.

Group or personal process

Action: As a group, list the principles that Pope Francis has outlined here and give one or two examples of how each plays a role in evangelization.

....

Discuss: Choose one principle from this list and talk about how you will implement it in your parish or other community.

IV. SOCIAL DIALOGUE AS A CONTRIBUTION TO PEACE

238 In order to succeed at speaking about our faith while we invite others and welcome them to join us, there must be dialogue in three forms: dialogue between the Church and various governments; dialogue with society, including academics and cultures; and dialogue with people who are not Catholic. 239. The Church proclaims the Gospel of peace and we wish to build a consensus on the urgency of this for all humanity. All the people of the earth must be included. 240. The state has a key role in this. 241. In entering into dialogue, the Church doesn't have every solution but wants to be a partner in the process.

242 We know that sometimes there seems to be no agreement between faith and science, but we propose instead that we dialogue together with an eye to agreeing on a synthesis. We trust reason and science because

they come from God. 243. The Church supports the advance of science and sees it as realizing the enormous potential that is God-given.

244 Likewise, we are committed to ecumenical dialogue. Our impact on the world would be so much greater if we were more unified. We are, after all, all pilgrims on the journey of faith. 245. Ecumenism is part of the march toward peace. 246. Our divisions as Christians are a scandal that impede our work. If we concentrate on what unites us and keep in mind that some truths are more central than others, we can open doors to one another. By talking together we can learn from each other. We have much to learn!

247 We also hold the Jewish people in special regard. The gifts that God has given to them have never been taken back. For us Christians, Judaism is not a foreign religion; we share belief in one God. 248. We regret the terrible persecutions of the Jews brought about by Christians. 249. Even though we feel we must proclaim Jesus as Messiah, there is nonetheless a rich array of values, beliefs, and convictions that we share.

250 If we are to achieve world peace, then we must also be in constant dialogue with the people of other non-Christian religions. We must be open to them and share their joys and sorrows. 251. In this dialogue, all parties must remain steadfast in their own convictions while sharing the common aim of peace, harmony, respect, and mutual enrichment.

252 The people of Islam now live throughout the world, and our dialogue with them is important. We also share one faith in God. We share many elements of our ethics. 253. In order for us to dialogue well, training is needed so we can all be grounded in our own identity while opening the door to each other. Muslin immigrants should certainly be welcomed in mainly Christians nations, and we also ask that Christians be likewise welcome in mainly Muslim places. We have all sometimes resorted to violence but both the Koran and the Gospels are opposed to every form of it.

254 In sum, non-Christians who follow their conscience are justified by the grace of God. God works in them, and their contributions to human life also enrich us.

255 We believe in religious freedom as a fundamental element of human rights. This includes the freedom to choose the religion one will follow. We respect this pluralism that values differences and believe that it does not require that all expressions of faith be within a church, synagogue, or mosque. 256. We should avoid crude and superficial generalizations about religions. Not all believers or leaders are alike. We should also respect thinking and writing that emerges from religious belief; not everything in society must be purely secular.

257 We also feel close to those who follow no religion whatsoever yet sincerely seek truth, beauty, and goodness. These are our allies and friends as we seek to defend human dignity and protect the environment. Dialogue with them is going on now and is a part of the path toward peace.

258 "Starting from certain social issues of great importance for the future of humanity, I have tried to make explicit once again the inescapable social dimension of the Gospel message and to encourage all Christians to demonstrate it by their words, attitudes and deeds."

Group or personal process
Discuss: Talk together about how dialogue plays a role in bringing about peace and justice?

....

Action: Could you and your community be in better dialogue? Plan ways to widen the dialogue you have with non-Catholics who may live within the households or neighborhoods of your community.

CHAPTER FIVE

Spirit-filled Evangelizers

259 *The Holy Spirit gives us the courage to proclaim fearlessly what we believe, both with words and with lives lived convincingly. 260. Here are some thoughts, now, about this work.*

261 *Spirit-filled people do not speak of their faith or invite others to join them because it is their mere duty. They do so because it is in their heart and they can't resist speaking about it. Let us invite the Spirit to fill us now.*

I. REASONS FOR A RENEWED MISSIONARY IMPULSE

262 If we do not spend considerable time with the Lord, meditating on his word and being surrounded by his presence, we cannot reach out to others. We must be people of pious faith. But we cannot become so involved in our prayer that we fail to act! 263. The early Christians knew this but every age has its share of difficulties. We should see our challenges today as different but still able to be met.

264 The reason we speak of our faith is because we are loved by Jesus. Only by his grace will our hearts be opened. When he touches us with grace, we are made new. This is at the basis of all we do. We share with others what we ourselves have experienced. Wonderful! 265. Jesus' self-giving love and attention to the poor reveal the mystery of God to us. This is what we now give witness to. By our own encounter with Christ, we become convinced of his love, and that conviction is what we speak about to others.

266 We are always disciples, always being renewed in our encounter with Christ. It is not something we experience once for all time, but an ongoing, ever-deeper intimacy with the person of Jesus Christ. He is at the heart of our missionary discipleship. 267. We are seeking in this what Jesus sought, namely, the glory of the Father (Ephesians 1:6).

268 We must also remain close to people's real lives. Our passion is for Christ but also for the people of Christ. 269. Jesus himself is the model of this. His entire ministry was about people. He looked into their eyes, touched them with his hands, and ate and drank with them. He gave himself for us people, which led to his self-emptying act on the cross. We likewise should move into society and out of our churches. We should rejoice with the happy and weep with the sad.

270 We need not keep the Lord's wounds at arm's length but should lean into human suffering and misery to give it meaning and purpose and to bring it to an ultimate end. 271. With gentleness and reverence (1 Peter 3:15) we give reasons for our own hope, our own happiness. We do not want to appear better than others, but to work with humility as Jesus did. We must stand among the people of God as servants. This isn't the pope's idea; it's embedded in the Scriptures we all hold dear.

272 Walking in love with our sisters and brothers is how we walk with

God. Indeed, not to have love plunges us into darkness (1 John 2:11). Our love can light up the whole world with hope! It is love in reality, not merely expressed as an ideal. This means it is love that translates itself into feeding the poor, loving the prisoner, and freeing those bound up by selfishness or greed. When we love others like this, we grow in our own faith. We are happy. Our happiness is contagious. Our hearts are open and we are free to love. What a great freedom this is!

273 As a Christian, this love isn't a mere job, something we can leave behind at "closing time." We live this love 24 hours per day, 7 days per week. People see us as nurses with real heart, teachers with heart, parents with heart. 274. We begin to see that every single person is worthy of our self-giving love. Every human being reflects God. We are God's people. Wonderful!

275 Earlier in this exhortation, I reflected on pastoral workers who lack deep spirituality. They give up, thinking that losing their comfort, time, or pride isn't worth the effort. But now we see that Christ is at the heart of it all. We are invited to encounter him, and through him we love others. 276. The resurrection is still happening today; where we might see only signs of poverty, death, destruction, hatred, and darkness, suddenly, because of us, a new light shines and it is the light of Christ coming through us.

277 We might not feel full satisfaction, but we can trust that, no matter what, love will be stronger than hate, light will conquer darkness, and our struggle will pay off. 278. The seeds of a new world are already planted and will grow into a great hope for all of humankind. 279. We cannot always see these seeds but we know God is with us. None of our acts of love will be lost; God will work through them all. Even if our efforts seem to yield no fruit, yet the seed is there and we must trust that the Spirit is with us.

280 We must trust this Spirit entirely. Place yourself in the Spirit's presence often. Open your heart. You will be led as God wills. 281. As we pray for others' needs, we find that the presence of God grows within us and our own needs are met. 282. We then pray with gratitude, for we have seen great and powerful divine love. We become bold because we have no more fear. 283. Such prayer leads us to see and love anew.

Group or personal process

Discuss: How does your personal faith show itself to others? How do you keep your own heart on fire with love?

....

Action: Plan ways your parish can help its members grow in their faith. Plan ways you could help members of the parish who have never had an initial encounter with Christ.

II. MARY, MOTHER OF EVANGELIZATION

284 Mary is also present to us as we speak of our faith and invite others to join us. 285. Jesus gave his mother to us while he was on the cross. "Here is your mother," he said (John 19:27). Let us receive her with open arms. Mary was the first missionary disciple. She is, indeed, our Mother. 286. Mary turned a humble stable into a temporary home for Jesus. She is a sign of hope for us; she opens our hearts; she shared our struggles, and in the end, she leads us to Christ. 287. Now we ask the Mother of Jesus to guide our hands and feet, to help us proclaim our faith and to invite and welcome in the name of Christ. 288. Mary's love and tenderness becomes the very style with which we now proclaim the good news that she bore in her own body. Her humility becomes our goal. Her faith is our faith.

She praised God for "bringing down the mighty from their thrones" and "sending the rich away empty-handed" (Luke 1:52–53). She pondered the mysteries of the faith in her heart. And in the end, she stood faithfully at the foot of the cross. With her, we now hear the words of the Risen Christ, "Behold, I make all things new" (Revelation 21:5).

Prayer: Working as a group, write a prayer that expresses your hopes and desires for living according to Pope Francis' message in this exhortation.